"Young families today want to celebrate the Savi[or] ... meaningful way—a new way! Barbara Reaoch [offers the] perfect package of fresh ideas in this excellent book. The colorful illustrations, interactive projects, family discussion points, and stories focus every member of the family on the extraordinary gifts that Jesus Christ brought with him when he came to earth. As you prepare for the Advent season, consider this unique book as your Christmas toolbox. I give it my double thumbs-up!"

JONI EARECKSON TADA, Joni and Friends International Disability Center

"Another outstanding family devotional by Barbara Reaoch. She has a knack for starting with something interesting to children and quickly turning it to Jesus and the Bible. The book is imaginatively interactive as well: not just something for kids to listen to. Best of all is how she conveys 25 core truths about Christ to show the children how Jesus is *Better Than Anything*."

DONALD S. WHITNEY, Professor of Biblical Spirituality and Associate Dean, The Southern Baptist Theological Seminary, Louisville, KY; Author, *Spiritual Disciplines for the Christian Life, Praying the Bible,* and *Family Worship*

"Would you like to offer your family an escape from the rush and crush of Christmas? That's exactly what Barbara Reaoch's new family devotional will help you do! *A Better Than Anything Christmas* shows us how to lead our children to the One who is better than anything that a Christ-less Christmas tries to offer. With simple—but profound—ways to gather around relevant Scriptures, along with age-appropriate questions and activities, Barbara's book helps us discover together all the 'betters' that Jesus came to give. I can't wait to use this with the children in my life!"

JANI ORTLUND, Renewal Ministries

"Families will love reading this 25-day Advent devotional together! With daily Bible discussion, interactive questions, and lots of extra activities, this book will light up your children's eyes and bring joy to your heart. Drawing on decades of experience, Barbara Reaoch beautifully uses simple language to paint deep truth. Simply charming."

CHAMP THORNTON, Pastor; Author, *The Radical Book for Kids* and *Why Do We Say Good Night?*

"It's December again. Christmas is just around the corner. Gather your family around. Open up this book. And get ready to celebrate the amazing gift of Jesus and the blessings he brings to us, not only at Christmas but year round! There truly is nothing (and no one!) better."

NANCY DEMOSS WOLGEMUTH, Author; Founder and Teacher, *Revive Our Hearts*

"This is a fantastic devotion for families! Its clear explanations, relatable seasonal illustrations and differentiated questions mean I have no doubt that young and old will be thrilled when they see again and again—and AGAIN—why Jesus really is the very best. The truths certainly made my heart sing!"

TAMAR POLLARD, Author, *Epic Explorers* and *One Day Wonders*

"This little book turns our eyes towards the amazing gift of Jesus at Christmas in a beautifully simple way, yet with enough depth that even older children and adults can be drawn to deeper faith and worship. I'm already thinking about who I might give a copy to!"

ALI CAMPBELL-SMITH, Youth Worker, Eden Baptist Church, Cambridge, UK

"Barbara does an outstanding job of keeping the focus on the centrality of Jesus in 25 of his incomparable gifts, the main and best gift being himself. The personalized artwork your children will add could make this book a family heirloom, revisited by your children's children."

SAM CRABTREE, Pastor, Bethlehem Baptist Church; Author, *Practicing Affirmation: God-Centered Praise of Those Who Are Not God*

"I look forward to sharing this book with the family this Christmas, most especially for how it promotes theologically robust discussion and a deepening and enduring understanding of God's word. From toddlers to teens, this devotional offers all children far greater value than even the most beautifully wrapped packages beneath the tree."

TARYN HAYES, Author, *Seekers of the Lost Boy*; Podcast Co-host, *The Lydia Project: Conversations with Christian Women* (The Gospel Coalition Australia)

"An enjoyable, attainable, and theologically rich family devotional. No need to gather glue sticks and glitter or find a spare hour—just gather the family on the couch and follow the short, simple structure toward 25 days of engaging, Christ-centered family worship."

LINDSEY CARLSON, Author, *Growing in Godliness: A Teen Girl's Guide to Maturing in Christ*; pastor's wife; mom of five

"More than anything, I want my children to walk away from our Advent season with a bigger, better view of our Savior, and Barbara's devotions help them do just that. If you're new to celebrating Advent, *A Better Than Anything Christmas* equips you with everything you need to begin."

GLENNA MARSHALL, Author, *The Promise is His Presence* and *Everyday Faithfulness*

BARBARA REAOCH

A
BETTER THAN
ANYTHING
CHRISTMAS

EXPLORE HOW JESUS MAKES

CHRISTMAS BETTER

thegoodbook
COMPANY

*To our grandchildren Milaina, Noah, Annalyse, Micah, Toph,
Judah and Hadassah that you may know "the praiseworthy
deeds of the L*ORD*, his power, and the wonders he has done."
Psalm 78 v 4-7*

A Better Than Anything Christmas
© Barbara Reaoch 2020

Published by:
The Good Book Company

thegoodbook.com | thegoodbook.co.uk
thegoodbook.com.au | thegoodbook.co.nz | thegoodbook.co.in

Cover design and illustrations by Emma Randall | Design and art direction by André Parker

ISBN: 9781784985301 | Printed in Turkey

CONTENTS

BEFORE YOU BEGIN

These devotions are ideal for all ages. They are about faith—trusting Jesus, not your own goodness. They are about repentance—living for Jesus, not yourself. They are for children who already believe and for those who do not yet believe in Jesus. We all need encouragement all the time to believe Jesus's truth.

Prepare your own heart before you lead your family or others in *A Better Than Anything Christmas*. Ask your heavenly Father to guide you. Ask for insight about what questions to ask and how to promote discussion. Pray for God to give you a daily desire to make Jesus the focus of this Christmas.

THE DAILY PATTERN

Each day has four parts: Explore, Explain, Engage, and Enter in. These are followed by a wonderful true statement about Jesus and some family journaling space.

EXPLORE

Reading the Bible passage together is the key activity. Why was Jesus born? God gives us his answer to this question in the Gospel accounts in Matthew, Mark, Luke, and John.

EXPLAIN

We usually think of Christmas as a time to make our own wish list and give gifts to others. The Bible tells us that Christmas is about the gifts Jesus came to give us! *A Better Than Anything Christmas* explores 25 gifts that Jesus's life gives us. All of Jesus's gifts are better than the best gifts we could ever ask for.

ENGAGE

There are two Engage questions for older children. The first helps children discover how each truth intersects with their lives. The second question stimulates deeper discussion.

Each Engage question also has a simpler version after it. This is ideal for younger children or those with less Bible knowledge. The older and younger questions are marked as shown below:

 For older children    For younger children

Be prepared to get the conversation going. Ask God for willingness to talk about times when you are tempted to sin. Pray that you will respond to your kids with understanding and not in a judgmental tone. As your family responds honestly to God's word and Spirit, they will begin to treasure the truth of Jesus.

ENTER IN

This short prayer is a springboard for your response to whatever God shows you about himself, Jesus, and yourself. The journal notes and pictures you make will continue to remind you of how God has used his Spirit and his word to work eternal miracles in your family.

JESUS IS…

These "Jesus is…" statements will help your family to remember that Christmas is about Jesus. Some have been decorated for you, though your child may want to add extra stars and patterns. Others have letter outlines for your child to color in.

FAMILY JOURNALING SPACE

This is a place to respond to what God has shown you. You might want to write down what you have learned, draw a picture, list things to thank God for, draw how your face looks when you think about Jesus, or use this space for any other way you want to respond to God. There is some extra journaling space at the back of the book for any days when you have an idea that needs more room.

ANSWERS

If you would find it helpful, you can download an answer sheet to all of the Explore and Engage questions from **www.thegoodbook.com/betterthan-answers.pdf**

TIPS FOR SUCCESS

Be brief. Be real. Be consistent.

SOME USEFUL BIBLE WORDS

AMEN: This Hebrew word means "I agree." It is a way of joining in with someone's prayer.

ANGEL: Angels are messengers from God.

BIBLE / SCRIPTURE / GOD'S BOOK: Although the Bible was written by about 40 people, God made sure that they wrote exactly what he wanted them to write. God speaks to us through the Bible, and what he says in the Bible is always true.

CHRISTMAS: We don't know exactly when Jesus was born, but December 25th was chosen as a day to celebrate Christmas—the birth of Jesus Christ.

FULFILLED: When one of God's promises is fulfilled, it means that he has done exactly what he promised to do. When Jesus was born at the very first Christmas, he fulfilled many of God's promises.

GOSPEL: The Greek word "gospel" means "good news." The gospel of Jesus is the good news that Jesus came to save us from the problem of sin.

IMMANUEL: This name for Jesus means "God with us."

KINGDOM OF GOD: This isn't a physical place. It is God's people living under his rule as their King.

MERCY: Mercy is when God doesn't treat us in the way we deserve. Instead God shows us grace, which is his huge kindness to people who don't deserve it.

MESSIAH / CHRIST: "Messiah" is a Hebrew word. The same word in Greek is "Christ." They both mean "the anointed one." When someone became king, they were anointed with oil. The names Messiah and Christ tell us that Jesus is God's chosen King.

REDEEM: To buy back or pay the price. Jesus came to redeem people by paying the price to rescue them from their sin.

RESURRECTION: Jesus died on the first Good Friday. But he didn't stay dead! On the first Easter Sunday God raised Jesus back to life.

RIGHTEOUS / RIGHTEOUSNESS: To be righteous means to be "right with God."

SIN / SINFUL: When we sin, we do what **we** want instead of what **God** wants. Jesus came to rescue us from the problem of sin.

SON OF MAN: A title Jesus often used for himself.

SPIRIT / HOLY SPIRIT: There is only one God, but he is three persons: God the Father, God the Son (Jesus), and God the Holy Spirit. The Spirit points us to the truth about Jesus, and helps us to live the way God's word (the Bible) tells us to.

THE CROSS: Jesus's enemies killed him by nailing him to a cross and leaving him there to die. But it was God who had already planned that Jesus would die. As Jesus died on the cross, he took all the punishment for our sin, so that everyone who trusts in Jesus can be forgiven.

DECEMBER 1ST
ALL GOD'S PROMISES

EXPLORE

Read Luke 1 v 26-33

What words are used to tell us about Mary? (verses 26-30)

What promises from God did the angel give Mary? (verses 31-33)

EXPLAIN

At Christmas, we want all our dreams to come true. We hope everyone keeps their promises. But even our best friends can't always keep their promises. It hurts when a promise is broken. God is not like that. Nothing will stop God from keeping his promises. *Jesus came to give us something better than a best friend's promise.*

Mary had questions. How could she be a mother? Why would God choose a poor girl to be the mother of God's Son? The angel told Mary, "No word from God will ever fail" (Luke 1 v 37). Whatever God promises will happen. We do not have to see it before we believe God.

God kept his promise to Mary. Mary's baby Jesus is the Word from God that never fails. Jesus makes all God's promises real to us. Through Jesus's life, death on the cross, and resurrection to newness of life, we know that God alone has all power to keep all his promises. The Bible tells us that "no matter how many promises God has made, they are 'Yes' in Christ" (2 Corinthians 1 v 20). **Christmas says that Jesus came so that all of God's good promises come true.**

ENGAGE

⭐ Why is God's promise of Jesus a "better than ever" promise?

_____

_____

_____

⭐ How do we know that God always keeps his promises?

_____

_____

_____

⭐ What do God's promises mean for your life?

_____

_____

_____

⭐ Where do we find God's promises?

_____

_____

_____

ENTER IN

Father God, you are always true to your word. Thank you for sending Jesus. We know that you alone have all power to keep all your promises. Help us to know you and love you more this Christmas and always. Amen.

JESUS IS GOD'S BEST EVER
PROMISE

FAMILY JOURNALING SPACE

IDEAS: Draw the angel telling Mary about Jesus; or write your own prayer; or something else…

DECEMBER 2ND
THE PURPOSE OF LIFE

EXPLORE

Read Luke 1 v 34-38

How did the angel answer Mary's question? (verses 35-37)

_____

_____

What was Mary's answer to the angel? (verse 38)

_____

_____

_____

EXPLAIN

Do we use Christmas ornaments to wear as clothes? No! We use ornaments to decorate a Christmas tree. Are sweet treats made to clean the floor? No! Sweet treats were made to eat. Do you know that _you_ have a purpose too? Our lives will always be less than best until we know that God made us for himself. _Jesus came to give us something better than living for ourselves._

Suddenly, Mary understood her purpose: "I am the Lord's servant … May your word to me be fulfilled," she said. We find true happiness in showing how great and good God is in whatever he calls us to do. This is called "glorifying God." Living for God gives him glory and us joy!

Through Mary's life, God planned to show his greatness and goodness. Jesus came to show us God exactly. When we see Jesus, we see God. Jesus said to his Father, "I have brought you glory on earth by finishing the work you gave me to do" (John 17 v 4). You were made for this purpose—to know, love, and glorify God as your Father. **Christmas says that Jesus came to give us our purpose.**

ENGAGE

What would you tell a friend who thinks "living for ourselves" is the purpose of life?

What was God's purpose for Mary?

We know God, love him, and glorify him as we read God's word, pray, and live for him. How will you plan, this month, to know, love, and glorify God?

For what purpose did God make you?

ENTER IN

Dear Jesus, your life gives our lives purpose. You made us to know you, love you, and glorify you. Help us to want to live for you and know true happiness. Show us what to stop doing so that we can start reading God's word and praying every day. Amen.

✦ LIVING FOR JESUS IS OUR PURPOSE ✦

FAMILY JOURNALING SPACE

IDEAS: Draw Mary as the Lord's servant; or list some things that give God glory and us joy; or something else…

DECEMBER 3RD
GOD'S AMAZING MERCY

EXPLORE

Read the start of Mary's song in Luke 1 v 46-52

What did Mary know about herself? (verse 48)

_____

_____

What did Mary know about God? (verses 50-52)

_____

_____

_____

EXPLAIN

Who is on your Christmas list? Have you ever decided not to give a good gift to someone who hurt your feelings? We often want to give the best gifts to people who are nice to us. God is not like that. God is merciful. He does not give us what our sins deserve. _Jesus came to give us something better than the best gifts we give._

No one has perfect thoughts, feelings or actions. No one obeys God completely. On our own we can't escape sin's punishment, which is death. Mary knew she had not earned God's love. With wonder-filled fear in God, Mary sang, "His mercy extends to those who fear him."

God, in mercy, sent Jesus to take the punishment for our sin. Proud people think they are good enough. They think they don't need the gift of Jesus's forgiveness. But God forgives all who in wonder-filled fear turn from sin and trust in Jesus. Jesus said, "I desire mercy, not sacrifice. For I have not come to call the righteous, but sinners" (Matthew 9 v 13). **Christmas says that Jesus came to give us God's mercy.**

ENGAGE

★ Do you think God forgives us because we do something good to make up for the bad things we have done? Why/why not?

_____

_____

_____

★ What does it mean that God is merciful?

_____

_____

★ Why is God's mercy such an amazing gift?

_____

_____

_____

★ Who did God send to take the punishment for our sin?

_____

_____

_____

ENTER IN

Father God, you are so merciful. You sent Jesus for us, knowing we could never do enough good to deserve forgiveness. Thank you, Jesus, for taking the punishment we deserve. We need a wonder-filled fear of you. Give us faith to turn away from sin and to trust in Jesus. Amen.

JESUS GIVES US GOD'S MERCY

FAMILY JOURNALING SPACE

IDEAS: Draw Mary singing; or write your own song of thanks to God; or something else…

DECEMBER 4TH

HUNGRY HEARTS

EXPLORE

Read the rest of Mary's song in Luke 1 v 53-55

What does God do for those who are hungry? (verse 53)

_____

_____

_____

What happens to the rich (prideful)? (verse 53)

_____

_____

_____

EXPLAIN

What yummy treats do you like to eat at Christmas? Just thinking about a favorite chocolate, fruit, or cake can make us hungry. Filling up with water does not stop our hunger for a treat. Our hearts get hungry, too. God gives us hearts that hunger for him. Stuffing our hearts with friendships, good grades, and even happy times at Christmas does not satisfy our hunger for God. *Jesus came to fill our hearts with something even better.*

Our friends, parents, family, sports, and talents are good gifts. But God did not design these gifts to be our greatest happiness. Mary said, "He has filled the hungry with good things." God fills our hearts with Jesus—the most satisfying food of all!

Jesus came to make our hearts his home. He said, "On that day you will realize that I am in my Father, and you are in me, and *I am in you*" (John 14 v 20). Because Jesus is in us, he gives our hearts new desires to love and please God. He even gives us a new ability to obey him. **Christmas tells us that Jesus came to fill our hearts with himself.**

ENGAGE

In what way do people try to fill their hungry hearts? Now be honest with yourself... What hunger is in your life?

_____

_____

_____

Why does God give us hungry hearts?

_____

_____

A heart filled with Jesus overflows! How will you share the love of Jesus this Christmas?

_____

_____

_____

How do we know that Jesus came to make our hearts his home?

_____

_____

ENTER IN

Father God, you kindly give us good gifts. We admit that we often act as if we need these gifts, and more of them, to make us happy. Help us to see that a heart filled with Jesus is better. Give us new desires to love God and live for him. Amen.

JESUS FILLS OUR HEARTS WITH HIMSELF

FAMILY JOURNALING SPACE

IDEAS: Draw what it might look like for God's word to feed us; or write how you feel about Jesus making his home in your heart; or something else…

DECEMBER 5TH

FULLY FREE

EXPLORE

Read the start of Zechariah's song in Luke 1 v 68-75

What did God do for his people? (verse 68)

Who did God rescue us from and why? (verse 74)

EXPLAIN

Freedom from school and homework! What will you do with your Christmas holiday free time? Freedom seems fun until we get bored. We can't find a friend to play with. We get into trouble. We can't really be free until we are free from sin. Here's good news: *Jesus came to give us freedom better than free time.*

Zechariah said this about the freedom Jesus gives: "Praise be to the Lord, the God of Israel, because he has come to his people and redeemed them" (Luke 1 v 68). Satan, the worst bully in the world, tempted Adam and Eve to disobey God. They sinned and lost their freedom to be God's friends. They no longer enjoyed obeying God. They could no longer fully obey God even when they wanted to. And every person after them has learned how strong sin is!

Jesus came to redeem us from our sin. "Redeem" means that Jesus paid the price to rescue everyone who believes in him from sin's strong grip. Jesus, our Redeemer, says, "So if the Son sets you free, you will be free indeed" (John 8 v 36). **Christmas says that Jesus came to give us freedom.**

ENGAGE

What freedom did we all lose after Adam and Eve's sin?

Who tempted Adam and Eve?

How is the freedom that Jesus gives us better than free time?

How can we be free from sin?

ENTER IN

Praise be to the Lord, for sending Jesus our Redeemer! Now we can enjoy true freedom. Help us to want to be free from sin's strong grip in our lives. Let us be free to enjoy your love and friendship. Amen.

JESUS BRINGS
FREEDOM

FAMILY
JOURNALING
SPACE

IDEAS: Draw what the freedom Jesus gives us looks like; or write
a list of words that mean the same as "redeem"; or something else…

DECEMBER 6TH
FULL FORGIVENESS

EXPLORE

Read the rest of Zechariah's song in Luke 1 v 76-79

What would Zechariah's son John tell the people? (verse 77)

_____

_____

_____

Why does God give his people forgiveness of their sins? (verse 78)

_____

_____

_____

EXPLAIN

Has an illness ever ruined your Christmas? Nobody wants medicine instead of gifts! Could anything be worse? Yes! Sin infects our hearts. Sin ruins more than our fun. Sin ruins our desire to love and obey God. Sin is not like catching a cold. We are all born with sin. And no medicine can make us better. _Jesus came with a gift better than medicine._

Zechariah's son, John, would tell people about Jesus's "salvation through the forgiveness of their sins" (v 77). God gives us the best gifts but sin ruins our hearts. So we say to God, "Go away! We don't want your gifts or you!" But God doesn't take his gift and go away.

If you hurt someone's feelings, you might want to give them a gift to say, "I'm sorry." What if the person you hurt gave *you* a gift? You would be amazed! God sent his best gift to us—his Son! Jesus heals our hearts so that we can love and trust God. "The Son of Man has authority on earth to forgive sins" (Mark 2 v 10). **Christmas says that Jesus came to give us forgiveness.**

ENGAGE

⭐ What makes God's gift of Jesus so amazing?

⭐ What would Zechariah's son John tell people about Jesus?

⭐ Sometimes we have a hard time asking for Jesus's forgiveness. Why do you think this is true?

⭐ Who did God send to forgive our sins?

ENTER IN

Father God, we admit there are times when we have acted as if we don't want your gifts or you. Please forgive us. Your gift of Jesus is better than anything. Jesus, we need you to heal our hearts so we can love and trust God. Amen.

✩ ✩ ✩ JESUS GIVES FORGIVENESS ✩ ✩ ✩

FAMILY JOURNALING SPACE

IDEAS: Draw what it means for our hearts to be healed; or write your own prayer; or something else…

DECEMBER 7TH
THE BABY WHO CAME TO SAVE

EXPLORE

Read Matthew 1 v 18-21

What did the angel tell Joseph? (verses 20-21)

_____

_____

_____

Why was Joseph to give the baby the name of Jesus? (verse 21)

_____

_____

EXPLAIN

Has your mom or dad ever rescued a Christmas gift you accidently lost? Accidents happen. Gifts get thrown out with Christmas wrapping paper. A lost gift cannot save itself. Someone must rescue it. The Bible says people are lost too. Who will find us and save us? _Jesus came to give us something better than ever—a gift we cannot lose._

Joseph was to name Mary's son Jesus, because "he will save his people from their sins." Only the perfect Jesus could take the punishment for sin we deserve. Jesus has always been fully God. He became a human baby for us. Like us, Jesus cried and was hungry. He had to learn to talk and walk and read God's word. As a child and as a man, Jesus was tempted to sin. Yet, Jesus never sinned. Jesus is the only human without sin.

Jesus died on the cross to give lost people a gift they cannot lose—forever life with God. Only Jesus can find us and take us to God. Jesus said this about himself: "For the Son of Man came to seek and to save the lost" (Luke 19 v 10). **Christmas says that Jesus came to rescue those who are lost.**

ENGAGE

⭐ Why is Jesus the only Person who can save lost people?

_____

_____

_____

⭐ Who is the only One who could take our punishment for sin?

_____

_____

_____

⭐ In your own words explain why Jesus came to seek and save the lost.

_____

_____

_____

⭐ What gift does Jesus give to those he saves?

_____

_____

_____

ENTER IN

Lord Jesus, you are fully God, yet you became a human baby for us. You fought every temptation we have, and yet never sinned. You alone can take us to God. It is awful to feel lost—but that is what we are without you. Please rescue each of us! Amen.

JESUS
RESCUES

FAMILY
JOURNALING
SPACE

IDEAS: Draw a picture of someone who was lost and
then found ; or write out Luke 19 v 10; or something else…

DECEMBER 8ᵀᴴ
GOOD NEWS

EXPLORE

Read Luke 2 v 8-12

What did the shepherds see and hear? (verses 8-10)

What good news did the angel tell the shepherds? (verse 11)

EXPLAIN

What is your favorite Christmas story? "Once upon a time" stories are fun, but *Jesus came to give us something better—God's one true Christmas story.* God promised to send his Messiah-King to rule the world. Jesus did not come as a king with jewels and palaces. Jesus came as a King to live in and rule our hearts, which are far more precious to him than jewels.

The angel told the shepherds, "Today in the town of David a Savior has been born to you; he is the Messiah, the Lord." King Jesus left behind his throne and the beauty of heaven. He lived and died a poor man to give us riches in his heavenly kingdom. As the King's children, one day we will rule with him in his kingdom forever.

Today, King Jesus lives in us and teaches us to love what he loves. Jesus said, "the kingdom of God is not coming in ways that can be observed ... the kingdom of God is in the midst of you" (Luke 17 v 20-21, ESV). **Christmas says that Jesus came to bring us into God's kingdom.**

ENGAGE

How is God's true Christmas story better than "once upon a time" stories?

How is Jesus different from other kings?

What is Jesus teaching you to love as he loves?

What does King Jesus teach his children?

ENTER IN

King Jesus, thank you for leaving your heavenly home to come to our home, so that we might be your children. Please rule in our hearts today and forever. We love many things, such as pizza, puppies and parties. But we want to learn to love what you love. Amen.

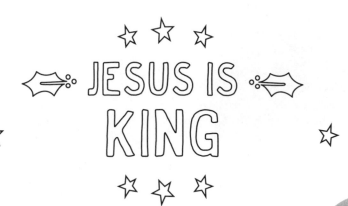

JESUS IS KING

FAMILY JOURNALING SPACE

IDEAS: Draw the beauty of Jesus' heavenly throne; or describe the kind of King that Jesus is; or something else…

DECEMBER 9TH
LOTS AND LOTS OF ANGELS

EXPLORE

Read Luke 2 v 13-14

What did the shepherds suddenly see and hear? (verses 13-14a)

What did the angels say would be given to God's children? (verse 14b)

EXPLAIN

At Christmas we try extra hard to speak kind words. No one wants fights at Christmas! When everyone is quiet it may seem like peace. But ignoring each other is not peace. Here's what we need: *Jesus came to give us peace that is even better than not fighting.*

The angels praised God and said, "Glory to God in the highest heaven, and on earth peace to those on whom his favor rests." Instead of loving God our Father, we often ignore him. But even if we try hard, we cannot make God have peace with us. God is just and holy. This means sinful people cannot come close to God. But God never stopped loving us! God sent his Son to take our sin and bring us to God. Now we can enjoy God's presence in safety.

Peace with God is his gift to all who turn from sin and trust in Jesus. We speak the kindest words of all when we tell others this good news of God's peace. Jesus said, "Peace be with you! As the Father has sent me, I am sending you" (John 20 v 21). **Christmas says that Jesus came to give us peace with God.**

ENGAGE

How is Jesus's peace better than trying to ignore God?

_____

_____

_____

What is God's gift to all who turn from sin and trust in Jesus?

_____

_____

_____

What can you tell a friend who thinks that being good means they have peace with God?

_____

_____

_____

What good news does Jesus give us to tell others?

_____

_____

_____

ENTER IN

Thank you, Jesus. Your life and death have given us the peace and friendship with God that we could never have on our own. Please show us someone who needs to hear this good news—that they too might enjoy peace with you this Christmas. Amen.

JESUS IS
PEACE

IDEAS: Draw the shepherds listening to the angels; or write "Glory to God" in bubble writing; or something else…

FAMILY
JOURNALING
SPACE

DECEMBER 10TH
THE GREATEST TREASURE

EXPLORE

Read Luke 2 v 15-20

What did the shepherds do after the angels left? (verses 15-18)

What did Mary do with all she heard about her child, Jesus? (verse 19)

EXPLAIN

Packages with bows on top promise Christmas happiness. But we sometimes fill our Christmas wishlist with gifts that cost more than our family can afford. When we don't get that high-priced gift, our hearts are filled with disappointment, not happiness. *Jesus came to give us a treasure better than the most expensive gift.*

Mary was poor. She had no gifts for her new baby. But God gave Mary a gift— Jesus, a treasure money cannot buy. "Mary treasured up all these things and pondered them in her heart." Why did angels and shepherds worship this baby? This gift of Jesus was so much more than Mary ever imagined. The excitement of a new Christmas gift becomes less day by day. But the gift of Jesus grows, the more we know and enjoy him.

Jesus tells us, "Where your treasure is, there your heart will be also" (Matthew 6 v 21). In Jesus, God welcomes us into his forever family. Jesus is the best gift of all. **Christmas says that Jesus came to give us the treasure of himself.**

ENGAGE

★ What are today's common treasures? How do we know what a person treasures the most?

_____

_____

_____

★ What gift did God give to Mary?

_____

_____

★ What sweet truths about Jesus are like a treasure chest to you?

_____

_____

_____

★ Who is God's best gift to us?

_____

_____

ENTER IN

Dear Jesus, you know everything about us, and you love us. We want to love you more. Please will you help us? Help us to love the truths of your life, death, and resurrection. As we read the Bible, help us to hold the sweet truths we read of you in our hearts forever. Amen.

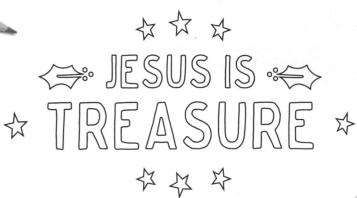

FAMILY
JOURNALING
SPACE

IDEAS: Draw the shepherds visiting baby Jesus; or draw/write
some sweet truths about Jesus; or something else…

DECEMBER 11TH
CLEAN CLOTHES

EXPLORE

Read Luke 2 v 22-24

What did the Law say Mary and Joseph must do with Jesus? (verses 22-23)

_____

_____

_____

Why did Joseph and Mary also offer a sacrifice? (verse 24)

_____

_____

_____

EXPLAIN

New clothes make great Christmas gifts! Looking good feels nice. But soon, lost buttons and food stains happen. _Jesus came to give us clothing better than our best._

Every day, Jesus thought and did everything right. He shared with his brothers and sisters. He obeyed his parents, and never argued or complained. He loved every word of God's Law. Mary and Joseph took Jesus to the temple "to present him to the Lord (as it is written in the Law of the Lord)". We may try hard. But we do not always love to obey. Even when others think we obey, sin stains our thoughts. In love, God sent Jesus to think, say, and do everything right for us.

When we trust Jesus as our Messiah-King, God counts Jesus's perfect "right-ness" as our own. Jesus's righteousness covers our sin-stained hearts. In Jesus, God welcomes us just as he welcomes his sinless Son. Jesus said, "Blessed are those who hunger and thirst for righteousness" (Matthew 5 v 6). Jesus gives us his clothes of righteousness (right-ness)—his perfectly right life. **Christmas says that Jesus came to give us his righteousness.**

ENGAGE

Why do you think obedience to parents, teachers and God is hard?

What did Jesus do right?

How can Jesus's perfect "right-ness" be your own?

What does God cover sin with?

ENTER IN

Dear Jesus, you kept every word of God's Law. You loved us enough to think, say, and do everything right for us. We want God to welcome us as he welcomes you. Please cover our sin-stained hearts with your perfect "right-ness." Amen.

JESUS IS RIGHTEOUS

FAMILY JOURNALING SPACE

IDEAS: Draw a picture of a clean heart; or list ways that sin stains our thoughts; or something else…

DECEMBER 12TH
SIMEON SEES THE SAVIOR

EXPLORE

Read Luke 2 v 25-32

What did Simeon know would happen before he died? (verse 26)

_____

_____

_____

Why did Simeon praise God when he saw Jesus? (verse 30)

_____

_____

_____

EXPLAIN

Seeing sparkling lights and ornaments tells us it's Christmastime. If the lights look blurry, we may need glasses. But even new glasses can't help us see the truth about Christmas. _Jesus came to give us something better than perfect eyesight._

When we place our trust in Jesus Christ, God gives us his Holy Spirit. The Holy Spirit gives us eyes to see God with our mind and heart. Simeon saw the baby Jesus. But the Holy Spirit gave him eyes to see the Messiah-King. He said, "My eyes have seen your salvation, which you have prepared in the sight of all nations."

No matter how big we grow, our minds are too small to know God. Jesus said, "Very truly I tell you, no one can see the kingdom of God unless they are born again" (John 3 v 3). Jesus came so that all God's children could know God. God gives all his children his Holy Spirit. The Holy Spirit shines light on God's word. With the Holy Spirit's help, we can know and love God's truth. **Christmas says that Jesus came to give us minds and hearts to see truth.**

ENGAGE

Why is knowing God different than knowing a subject in school?

What did Simeon know when he saw Mary's baby?

What do you think it means that "our minds are too small to know God"?

What does God give all his children so they know God's truth?

ENTER IN

Father God, thank you for sending Jesus to give us your Holy Spirit. We would not know you on our own. As we read the Bible, help us to see big truths about Jesus. We want to live with you in love and joy forever! Amen.

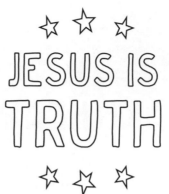

JESUS IS TRUTH

FAMILY JOURNALING SPACE

IDEAS: Draw Simeon in the temple; or write about a time when the Holy Spirit helped you know and love God's truth; or something else…

❄ DECEMBER 13ᵀᴴ ❄
TAKE HEART

EXPLORE

Read Luke 2 v 34-35

What did Simeon know about Jesus? (verse 34)

_____

_____

_____

What did Simeon say that Jesus knows about our hearts? (verse 35)

_____

_____

_____

EXPLAIN

Christmas tastes delicious! Imagine chocolates filled with caramel, fudge, or raspberry! Until we try one, we won't know if we picked our favorite filling or something we don't like. The first bite tells us the truth. Hearts have a filling, too. *Whatever we look like on the outside, Jesus came to fill our hearts with something better.*

Simeon's heart was filled with love and trust in the Messiah-King God had promised to send. Jesus is the Messiah-King. But not everyone believes this truth and trusts in Jesus. Simeon knew that Jesus came to tell us what fills our hearts. "This child is destined ... to be a sign ... so that the thoughts of many hearts will be revealed."

God knows all things. He knows our thoughts and our feelings. Jesus said, "Do not let your hearts be troubled. You believe in God; believe also in me" (John 14 v 1). Sin or fear or sadness may fill our hearts. But when we turn to Jesus, he rescues us. We taste his forgiveness, courage, and comfort. He fills our hearts with his Spirit and assures us we are God's children. **Christmas says that Jesus came to tell us the truth about our hearts.**

ENGAGE

⭐ What truth about your heart is God showing you?

_____

_____

_____

⭐ What does God know about us?

_____

_____

_____

⭐ In your own words describe why it is good to know the truth about our hearts.

_____

_____

_____

⭐ What truths about Jesus help you?

_____

_____

_____

ENTER IN

Father God, you know all our thoughts and feelings. You know when our hearts are filled with sin, fear, or sadness. Jesus, please help us to believe in you. We want to be your children. Please fill our hearts with yourself. Amen.

JESUS REVEALS WHAT'S IN OUR HEARTS

FAMILY JOURNALING SPACE

IDEAS: Draw Mary holding baby Jesus; or write about what God is revealing to you; or something else…

DECEMBER 14TH

RESCUE WHEN WE ARE TEMPTED

EXPLORE

Read Luke 2 v 36-38

What are at least three things God tells us about Anna? (verses 36-37)

What did Anna do after she thanked God for Jesus? (verse 38)

EXPLAIN

Christmas is fun. But Christmas temptations can hurt. When we are tempted, it's like putting on glasses that don't work. Our sin looks so small. But anger, greed, lies, and jealousy are huge. Everyone gets hurt! We might pretend we aren't tempted. *But Jesus came to give us something better than fake goodness.*

We all struggle to see our sin. Here's the best news ever—Jesus is ready to redeem us! This means Jesus rescues us so we no longer have to sin. We don't have to hurt ourselves and others anymore. Like Anna, we can pray. Jesus answers his children's prayers with the desire and strength to obey God. Anna saw Jesus and thanked God. She "spoke about the child to all who were looking forward to the redemption of Jerusalem."

Anna began to tell everyone this exciting news about Jesus! We don't have to be fooled by sin anymore. We don't have to fake goodness. Jesus keeps the true fun in Christmas. Jesus taught us to ask God to "Forgive us our sins ... and lead us not into temptation" (Luke 11 v 4). **Christmas says that Jesus came to redeem us from sin that tempts us.**

ENGAGE

What struggle with temptation and sin tries to hurt your Christmas?

What is Jesus ready to do with our sin?

What truths about Jesus keep the true fun in Christmas?

What can we do when we are tempted to sin?

ENTER IN

Father God, thank you for sending Jesus as our Redeemer. We don't always see our sin as easily as everyone else does. We need your help. Help us to remember to ask for the desire and strength to obey you. Amen.

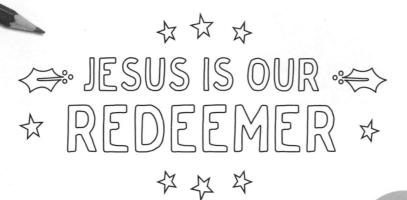

JESUS IS OUR REDEEMER

FAMILY
JOURNALING
SPACE

IDEAS: Draw Anna in the temple; or write your thoughts about a truly fun Christmas; or something else…

DECEMBER 15TH
GOD WITH US

EXPLORE

Read Matthew 1 v 22-23

What did the Lord say through the prophet? (verses 22-23)

_____

_____

_____

What does Immanuel mean? (verse 23)

_____

_____

_____

EXPLAIN

Who do you hope to visit this Christmas? _Jesus came to give us something better than a visit with our most favorite friend._ On the day Jesus was born, God himself came to be with us! No friend is better to be with than God. God showed his love by coming to be with us in his Son Jesus.

"The Lord had said through the prophet … 'they will call him Immanuel' which means 'God with us'" (Matthew 1 v 22-23). From before the world began, Jesus has always been God. He was born a real human baby to bring us to God. On the cross, he suffered the forever separation from God that our sin deserves. Now God is with all who trust in Jesus.

When Jesus was born, God came to make his home with us. Jesus said, "The one who loves me will be loved by my Father, and I too will love them and show myself to them" (John 14 v 21). God loves you more than you know. He wants to be with you and you to be with him. **Christmas says that Jesus came to give us God.**

ENGAGE

⭐ What truths about Jesus help you when you feel lonely?

⭐ Who became a real human baby to bring us to God?

⭐ Have you experienced what it's like to be far away from God and then be close to him? What is it like?

⭐ What did Jesus do so that we may be with God?

ENTER IN

Dear Jesus, thank you for suffering the forever separation from God that our sins deserve. We're amazed that God wants to be with us. We want to be close to God too. Amen.

JESUS IS GOD

FAMILY JOURNALING SPACE

IDEAS: Draw Jesus at home with you; or write
what it means to have Jesus close to you; or something else…

DECEMBER 16TH
KING OF KINGS

EXPLORE

Read Matthew 2 v 1-6

Why did the Magi come to Jerusalem? (verses 1-2)

_____

_____

_____

How did King Herod feel about the Magi's news? (verse 3)

_____

_____

_____

EXPLAIN

Santa gets lots of attention at Christmas. He's in shopping malls, at parties, on screens, and posters. Children praise Santa! They hope he'll keep his promises. _But there's One much better than Santa—One who is worthy of all our praise— Jesus our King!_

We learn to respect those in charge. But even the highest leader must honor Jesus! Jesus is the King above all kings. The Magi asked, "Where is the one who has been born king of the Jews? We saw his star when it rose and have come to worship him."

King Herod wanted people to praise him. But trying to make people respect and honor us can never make us truly happy. Jesus came to give his life to us. Now we can give all respect and honor to him. Life with King Jesus means praising him above all others. On the day Jesus returns, everyone will know him as King. "On his robe and on his thigh he has this name written: KING OF KINGS AND LORD OF LORDS" (Revelation 19 v 16). **Christmas says that Jesus came to give us joy in praising him as King.**

ENGAGE

★ How would you describe someone who wants everyone's attention and praise?

★ What did King Herod want?

★ Why do you think Jesus is worthy of all our praise?

★ Who is the King worthy of our praise?

ENTER IN

King Jesus, we praise you because you are the only one worthy of praise. Teach us what it means to worship you as our King. We want our lives to honor you. Please help us to know what to do and not do, that we might respect you with our words and choices. Amen.

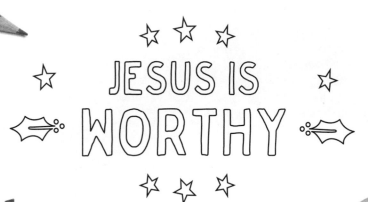

JESUS IS WORTHY

FAMILY JOURNALING SPACE

IDEAS: Draw a bright star; or write why Jesus is a King better than any other; or something else…

DECEMBER 17ᵀᴴ
GIFTS FOR THE KING

EXPLORE

Read Matthew 2 v 9-12

What did the Magi do first when they saw Jesus with Mary? (verse 11)

What gifts did the Magi give Jesus? (verse 11)

EXPLAIN

Where is your favorite gift from last Christmas? Has the joy from old Christmas gifts lasted? Often, clothes wear out, or toys break, and we lose interest. *Jesus came to give us something better than the joy of the best-ever Christmas gift.*

Wise men called Magi brought Jesus expensive gifts of gold, frankincense, and myrrh. They knew Jesus was the King and worthy of their best. "They saw the child with his mother Mary, and they bowed down and worshiped him." God made us to worship. Until we know Jesus, we worship other things—mostly ourselves. When we know Jesus, he fills our lives with worship of the one true God.

Jesus is worthy of our best gift. But Jesus did not come to *receive* gifts. He came to *give* us the best-ever gift. To all who trust him, Jesus gives a new heart that will praise him joyfully forever. Jesus said, "I have told you this so that my joy may be in you and that your joy may be complete" (John 15 v 11). **Christmas says that Jesus came to give us joy-filled worship that will last forever!**

ENGAGE

⭐ What truths about Jesus make you want to love him and live for him?

_____

_____

_____

⭐ What did the Magi do when they saw Jesus?

_____

_____

⭐ Jesus came to give you forever joy. Have you told him, "Jesus I trust you, please give me a new heart to love you and live for you"? If you have, then thank him for your new heart. If you haven't, would you like to pray that prayer now?

_____

_____

_____

⭐ What does God give to all who trust Jesus?

_____

_____

ENTER IN

Dear Jesus, you are worthy of the best gifts. Yet you are the Giver of a better-than-ever gift—yourself! We admit that our wishlists are filled with other gifts. Please give us new hearts to love you. Let us know your joy in our hearts today. Amen.

JESUS BRINGS JOY

FAMILY JOURNALING SPACE

IDEAS: Draw the Magi's gifts to Jesus; or write how the gift of Jesus is better than any other; or something else…

DECEMBER 18TH
ESCAPE TO EGYPT

EXPLORE

Read Matthew 2 v 13-16

Why did the angel tell Joseph to take Jesus to Egypt? (verse 13)

_____

_____

_____

Why was King Herod so angry? (verse 16)

_____

_____

_____

EXPLAIN

Herod doesn't fit our idea of Christmas fun. Can't we just forget about him? No! Because *Jesus came to give us something better than leaving Herod out of God's true Christmas story.*

"When Herod realized that he had been outwitted by the Magi, he was furious." Herod's evil anger wanted to get rid of Jesus. Evil tries to ruin God's good world. God built a beautiful garden for his first children, Adam and Eve. Evil led them to believe a lie instead of God's true word. The lie brought sin and death for

Adam, for Eve, and for us. Now, instead of loving and worshiping God, we love ourselves most of all.

Just like Herod, evil always tries to get rid of Jesus. But Jesus came to deliver us from evil. He beat death and evil with his life. Though Jesus's death was evil, through the cross he delivers us from sin and death. Jesus opened the way for us to be God's children and love him most of all. Jesus tells us to ask God to "deliver us from the evil one" (Matthew 6 v 13). **Christmas says that Jesus came to deliver us from evil.**

ENGAGE

How does evil try to get rid of Jesus today?

Who did Herod try to get rid of?

From what evil has Jesus delivered you?

How did Jesus beat sin and death?

ENTER IN

Lord Jesus, thank you for coming to deliver us—with your life and death. Help us to know when evil around us is trying to get rid of you. Please rid our hearts of evil so that we can love you more. Amen.

✫ ✫ ✫ JESUS IS OUR DELIVERER ✫ ✫ ✫

FAMILY JOURNALING SPACE

IDEAS: Draw the angel's visit to Joseph; or write your own prayer asking Jesus for help; or something else…

DECEMBER 19TH
NEW LIFE WITH GOD FOREVER

EXPLORE

Read John 1 v 1-4

Jesus is "the Word" in verse 1. Where was Jesus in the beginning? (verse 2)

_____

_____

_____

What is in Jesus that he gives to us? (verse 4)

_____

_____

_____

EXPLAIN

At Christmas we celebrate Jesus's birthday! But Jesus was alive as God's Son before time began. "He was with God in the beginning." With one mind and heart, the Father, Son, and Holy Spirit planned for _Jesus to leave his home in heaven to come and give us something better than anything!_

We celebrate the day we were born with parties and gifts. But all who believe and love Jesus have a better, forever birthday. God's children, born again into his forever family, receive a better gift. As soon as we become God's child, our forever life begins. God's gift of life never ends.

When Jesus died, parties and gifts seemed to be over forever. But after three days, Jesus was alive again! Sin and death lost. Jesus won new life for all God's children. Now, when God's children close their eyes in death, they wake up in heaven and see Jesus forever. Jesus tells us, "Everyone who looks to the Son and believes in him shall have eternal life, and I will raise them up at the last day" (John 6 v 40). **Christmas says that Jesus came to give us life forever with him!**

ENGAGE

⭐ How did Jesus win new life for all God's children?

⭐ What did Jesus win for all God's children?

⭐ Are you sure you are God's child? Jesus invites you to ask him for life that lasts forever. Will you write a prayer and ask God for faith to trust Jesus (for the first time), or to keep on trusting Jesus (if you're already God's child)? You might enjoy reading your prayer aloud to him.

⭐ How long do God's children live?

ENTER IN

Dear Jesus, thank you for beating death! You are stronger than the sin in our hearts. Please give us faith to turn from our sin and trust you. Make us children in your forever family. Amen.

JESUS IS
LIFE

FAMILY
JOURNALING
SPACE

IDEAS: Draw a birthday celebration; or write a thank-you note to Jesus for his gift of forever life; or something else…

DECEMBER 20TH
THE LIGHT IN JESUS

EXPLORE

Read John 1 v 1-5

What is Jesus's life to all mankind? (verse 4)

Is the darkness able to put out the light of Jesus? (verse 5)

EXPLAIN

Christmas lights are everywhere! All around, lights sparkle from trees, signs, buildings, and houses. But not even the brightest Christmas lights can give true light to our minds and hearts. *Jesus came to give us a better-than-ever light.* Jesus's light "shines in the darkness, and the darkness has not overcome it."

When Adam and Eve sinned, darkness fell on God's perfect world. Now earthquakes, hurricanes, and floods happen. People get sick. Darkness is everywhere, even in our hearts. Darkest of all was when wicked men killed Jesus. On the day Jesus died, the sun hid (Matthew 27 v 45). Would darkness last forever? Through his death on the cross, Jesus pushed away the darkness of sin and death.

Then Jesus rose from death! Jesus is the Light. He rescues God's children from darkness. Like the sun, his light gives life that makes us grow. His word shines into our hearts. His Spirit shines into our minds. His light shows us how to live and think. Jesus promises, "Whoever follows me will never walk in darkness, but will have the light of life" (John 8 v 12). **Christmas says that Jesus came to give us light.**

ENGAGE

⭐ Describe the difference between "darkness" and "the light of life."

⭐ What happened to God's perfect world when Adam and Eve sinned?

⭐ How have you seen Jesus as light in your life?

⭐ How did Jesus rescue God's children from darkness?

ENTER IN

Lord Jesus, you are light. Thank you for pushing away the darkness so that we can follow you. Please help us to love the light. We want to live in your light. Amen.

JESUS IS LIGHT

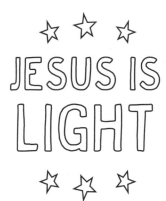

FAMILY JOURNALING SPACE

IDEAS: Draw the brightness of God's word shining in our hearts; or write about how you are seeing new things in God's word; or something else...

DECEMBER 21ST
THE TRUE STORY

EXPLORE

Read John 1 v 6-9

Why did God send John? (verses 6-7)

_____

_____

_____

Was John the light? (verses 8-9)

_____

_____

_____

EXPLAIN

Christmas movies old and new warm our hearts. What stories help your family to get ready for Christmas? Even our favorite movie or book does not tell the best story of all. _Jesus came to give us the gospel, his true story, which is better than any story ever told._ What is the gospel? It's the true story that God forgives our sin through Jesus's life, death, and resurrection.

God sent a man named John to help people get ready to hear the gospel. John "came as a witness to testify concerning that light, so that through him all might believe." Jesus is brighter than sunlight. He shows us the wrong things we think, say and do. So, when we hear Jesus's true story, we know that the gospel is the best news ever!

When we tell others the gospel, it honors Jesus and fills us with joy. Jesus said, "And the gospel must … be preached to all nations" (Mark 13 v 10). Faith in Jesus comes through hearing the true gospel. God's children turn to Jesus and receive all he has for them. **Christmas says that Jesus came to give us the gospel, his true story about forgiveness.**

ENGAGE

⭐ What did John know about Jesus that gave him courage to tell others the gospel truth?

⭐ Who did God send to help people get ready for Jesus?

⭐ What truth can you share with a friend who does not yet believe in Jesus?

⭐ What truth about Jesus do you want to tell your friend?

ENTER IN

Father God, help us to love the truth about Jesus. Give us faith to admit the wrong things we think, say, and do. We want to know the joy of your forgiveness. Please help us to share your true gospel story with our friends. Amen.

JESUS'S STORY IS TRUE

FAMILY JOURNALING SPACE

IDEAS: Draw John telling people about Jesus; or write a prayer for courage to share the gospel with a friend; or something else…

☀ DECEMBER 22ND ☀
THE BEST-EVER FAMILY

EXPLORE

Read John 1 v 9-13

What did Jesus give to all who believed in his name? (verse 12)

How are God's children born into his family? (verse 13)

EXPLAIN

Will you see a grandparent this Christmas? Will aunts, uncles, and cousins come to visit? No family is perfect, but God uses families to remind us of his love. *Jesus came to give us a family that is better than the best.* In Jesus's family, God is our Father, we are his children, and heaven is our home.

God created all people. But since Adam, many people are still separated from God by their sin. God graciously gives life, food, and everyday delights to all, but not everyone believes in his name. God lovingly sent Jesus to give us a new family, but not everyone wants to be God's child. Not everyone accepts God's gift of his forever family in Jesus.

Yet God rescues all who trust Jesus. "To those who believed in his name, he gave the right to become children of God." We can give our family and friends the best gift. When we tell them about Jesus, they can become God's children too.

Jesus said, "They are God's children, since they are children of the resurrection" (Luke 20 v 36). **Christmas says that Jesus came to give us a place in his family.**

ENGAGE

⭐ What truths about Jesus's family help you to love him even more?

_____

_____

_____

⭐ Does everyone receive God's gift of a forever family through Jesus?

_____

_____

_____

⭐ What could you say to a friend who is not sure they are God's child?

_____

_____

_____

⭐ Who is welcomed as God's child?

_____

_____

_____

ENTER IN

Lord Jesus, you came to give us the right to become God's children. Please give us faith to believe you are the Son of God. We want to be God's children in your family, forever. Amen.

☆ ☆ ☆
JESUS IS
FAMILY
☆ ☆ ☆

FAMILY JOURNALING SPACE

IDEAS: Draw a picture of God's family—people of all nations; or write a prayer asking God for the faith to become his child; or something else…

DECEMBER 23RD
GOD'S BEAUTY

EXPLORE

Read John 1 v 14-16

What do we see in Jesus? (verse 14)

Where did Jesus come from? (verse 14)

EXPLAIN

When you look at a present, are you able to guess what gift is underneath the wrapping? The full beauty of a gift stays hidden until we unwrap it. Is there anything better than finally tearing open the wrapping to see the gift inside? Yes! *Jesus came to give us something better!*

God is Spirit. We cannot see God. But God shows his beauty to us every day. All that God is—his power, mercy, grace, judgment, holiness, and love—show us his beauty. God shows his beauty through the world and the people he made. Everything we do—when we sing, play, learn, and are kind—can show us God's beauty. But Jesus fully unwraps God's beauty—his glory—for us to see. "We have seen his glory, the glory of the one and only Son, who came from the Father..."

We see God's beauty best by looking to Jesus's life, death, and resurrection. Jesus said to his Father, "I want those you have given me to be with me where I am, and to see my glory, the glory you have given me" (John 17 v 24). Excitement from gifts fades with time, but Jesus's beauty never fades. **Christmas says that Jesus came to show us God's beauty.**

ENGAGE

⭐ What truths about God's beauty make you want to live for him?

⭐ How does God show us his beauty every day?

⭐ How do God's children show Jesus's beauty to others?

⭐ Who unwraps God's beauty for us to see?

ENTER IN

Dear Jesus, when we see you, we see God. We want our friends to see your beauty. As others listen to what we say and watch the choices we make, let them be amazed, not with us, but with YOU! Amen.

JESUS IS
BEAUTIFUL

FAMILY JOURNALING SPACE

IDEAS: Draw the beauty of God in creation; or write a poem of how Jesus is the full beauty of God to you; or something else…

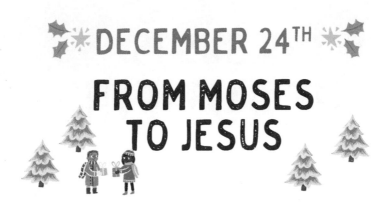

DECEMBER 24ᵀᴴ
FROM MOSES TO JESUS

EXPLORE

Read John 1 v 16-17

Who gave us God's law? (verse 17)

_____

_____

What did God give us through Jesus Christ? (verse 17)

_____

_____

EXPLAIN

What is the first thing to learn if you play a new game this Christmas? The rules! Rules are good. They help everyone play fairly. Cheating ends the fun. _Jesus came to give us something even better than the very best rules._ Jesus came to give us grace and truth.

God gave us his good rules through Moses. God was very kind when he gave the Law to Moses. As well as giving God's people rules to show them how to obey him, the Law also gave them a way to stay friends with him when they broke his rules. So the Law was amazing grace—undeserved kindness—from God. But we all cheat God! How could any of us really be his friends when we break his good rules? Here's how. The Law pointed forward to an even greater kindness from God: his Son. Jesus is the "grace" God gives us "in place of grace already given"—the Law.

Jesus is full of "grace and truth." He kept God's rules perfectly. He died so we can be forgiven and know we are friends with God forever. We don't pay for gifts we receive. The gift-giver pays. Jesus paid for God's gift to us. Jesus obeyed God's law, lived without sin, and died on the cross for us. Jesus said, "Whoever hears my word and believes him who sent me has eternal life" (John 5 v 24). This is the greatest truth in the world! And it is the most amazing grace ever given! Now God's Spirit lives in us and gives us the desire and strength to obey him. We can live as Jesus' friends, enjoy keeping his good rules, and know we are completely forgiven when we fail to. **Christmas says that Jesus came to give us the greatest grace and truth.**

ENGAGE

How does knowing that Jesus paid for God's gift to us help you to love him even more?

Who gave us God's good rules?

How do you see Jesus's truth and grace changing the way you speak and act?

Who gave us God's grace and truth?

ENTER IN

Father God, thank you for the good rules given through Moses. Lord Jesus, thank you for keeping all the good rules. You paid for God's gift to us. We need your grace and truth. Please grow our desire and strength to obey you. Amen.

✫ ☆ ✫
JESUS GIVES US GRACE
AND TRUTH
✫ ☆ ✫

FAMILY
JOURNALING
SPACE

IDEAS: Draw two gifts under a Christmas tree. Label one gift, GRACE and the other gift, TRUTH; or write a letter to a friend who thinks he or she has to earn God's love; or something else…

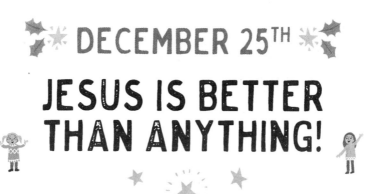

DECEMBER 25TH
JESUS IS BETTER THAN ANYTHING!

EXPLORE

Read John 1 v 18

Who has seen God? (verse 18a)

What kind of relationship does Jesus have with God? (verse 18b)

EXPLAIN

Don't you love a Christmas Day invitation! What fun to play games with friends and talk and eat together. Invitations are gifts of love. *Jesus came to give us an invitation better than all others.* He invites us to a better-than-anything life!

Jesus's life shows us that God knows us and loves us. Jesus knows God the way best friends know and love each other. In Jesus, God invites us into this better-than-best friendship. "No one has ever seen God, but the one and only Son, who is himself God and is in closest relationship with the Father, has made him known." God sees us every minute—both the good and the not-so-nice things we try to hide from others.

God knows the worst about us and yet never stops loving us. He gave his Son to die for you—to invite you to a holy and happy friendship with him, forever. Jesus said to his followers, "I no longer call you servants … Instead, I have called you friends, for everything that I learned from my Father I have made known to you" (John 15 v 15). **Christmas says that Jesus came to give us a better-than-anything life as God's friends!**

ENGAGE

In Jesus, God invites you to a better-than-best friendship forever! Will you receive his invitation?

_____

_____

_____

What does God know about us?

_____

_____

Christmas says Jesus came to give us _____. Fill in the blank with as many gifts as you remember.

_____

_____

_____

What invitation does Jesus give to God's children?

_____

_____

_____

ENTER IN

Take a few minutes to thank Jesus for coming to give you HIMSELF—the greatest gift.

JESUS IS BETTER THAN ANYTHING!

MERRY CHRISTMAS! This journaling space is for Christmas Day.

IDEAS: Draw an invitation (Who, What, Where) from God to you; or list some of the ways Jesus is better than anything; or something else...

EXTRA SPACE: This journaling space is for any day when you need more room.

FAMILY
JOURNALING
SPACE

EXTRA SPACE: This journaling space is for any day when you need more room.

FAMILY
JOURNALING
SPACE

EXTRA SPACE: This journaling space is for any day when you need more room.

THANK YOU

I'm indebted to my mentor and friend Sara Brigman, who taught me to write through her prayers, skill, and ability to taste the sweetness of Jesus in every passage.

I've benefited from the wisdom of my son Benjamin Reaoch, who gave this manuscript a thorough pastoral and theological review for accuracy.

I am grateful to Alison Mitchell, who believed in this book when it was just an idea. Her insights and editorial gifts have impacted my writing.

BAKE THROUGH THE BIBLE

Transform baking with your children into opportunities to teach the Bible!
These Bible overviews for pre-schoolers help parents with young children
to explore the Bible with their child while having lots of fun cooking
together. Written by Susie Bentley-Taylor and Bekah Moore.

thegoodbook.com/bttb
thegoodbook.co.uk/bttb

BIBLE-READING FOR EVERY AGE AND STAGE

Explore
(for adults)

Engage
(for 14+)

Discover
(for 11-13s)

XTB
(for 7-10s)

Table Talk
(for families)

Beginning with God
(for pre-schoolers)

thegoodbook.com/subscriptions
thegoodbook.co.uk/subscriptions

BIBLICAL | RELEVANT | ACCESSIBLE

At The Good Book Company, we are dedicated to helping Christians and local churches grow. We believe that God's growth process always starts with hearing clearly what he has said to us through his timeless word—the Bible.

Ever since we opened our doors in 1991, we have been striving to produce Bible-based resources that bring glory to God. We have grown to become an international provider of user-friendly resources to the Christian community, with believers of all backgrounds and denominations using our books, Bible studies, devotionals, evangelistic resources, and DVD-based courses.

We want to equip ordinary Christians to live for Christ day by day, and churches to grow in their knowledge of God, their love for one another, and the effectiveness of their outreach.

Call us for a discussion of your needs or visit one of our local websites for more information on the resources and services we provide.

Your friends at The Good Book Company

thegoodbook.com | thegoodbook.co.uk
thegoodbook.com.au | thegoodbook.co.nz
thegoodbook.co.in